THE CROSS
AND
THE PEACOCK

POEMS

THE CROSS
AND
THE PEACOCK

POEMS

BAIJU MARKOSE

2021

The Cross and the Peacock— Published by the Indian Society for Promoting Christian Knowledge (ISPCK), Post Box 1585, Kashmere Gate, Delhi-110006.

© Author, 2021

Cover page courtesy: Dharma Jyoti. Vidya Peeth, Faridabad

ISBN: 978-93-90569-40-3

Laser typeset and cover design by **ISPCK,** Post Box 1585, 1654 Madarsa Road, Kashmere Gate, Delhi-110006,
Tel: 23866323
e-mail– ashish@ispck.org.in   • ella@ispck.org.in
website-www.ispck.org.

Contents

Foreword

Dr. Baiju Markose is a thinker-feeler of great expansion. He is a powerful scholar and a wonderful poet. In this new beautiful book, "The Cross and the Peacock," Dr Markose shows us his gifted heart, opening ways for us to see the world, God, the earth and its creatures. Filled with surprises all along, each poem brightens the smallness of things and opens it all up in fullness. The poem that gives the title to the book, is an amazing rendering on the cross. Relating cross with feathers, water and more, the cross is drenched in human-animal-vegetal life. However, my favorite poem is Holy...Holy... Holy where getting dirt-ied with soil, washing dishes and playing with soap bubbles becomes whole/holy moments. I was blessed to read these poems and was left in awe with this book. We need more theologians/

poets like Dr. Markose, to help us see life, God and the earth in much more gentle, brighter ways.

Dr. Cláudio Carvalhaes,
Associate Professor of Worship,
Union Theological Seminary, New York, USA.

Preface

These poetic renderings are the thick descriptions of my own everyday-epiphanies! They have emerged out of the radical dis-enclosure of the socio-political-cultural-eco-system around us. To externalize my own sedimented silence deep within me, I found poetics as a way out! I hope these tiny but thick poetic descriptions will re-kindle your poetic and prophetic imaginations too. By interfacing the Cross and the Peacock, one of the poetic pieces in this collection, I try to posit Christ as the interlocutor between the world's terrible wounds and salvific wonder latent in our quotidian life. For me, poetry is not luxury, rather a disturbing and transposing act! A special word of thanks to Dr. Claudio Carvalhaes, Associate Professor of Worship, Union

Theological Seminary, New York for the foreword and the gracious words of endorsement.

Welcome to the uncharted terrain of theo-poetics!

– **Baiju Markose**

The Third-Shore

Two shores

of the same river

met at a third-space

under the water!

They said;

We are one!

In that third-shore

they found each other!

2

The Cross and the Peacock

In the Cross

I see a peacock

Plucking feathers

To preen and groom!

In the Cross

I smell the Animality

Unplugged in its beauty!

In the Cross

I see the Complexity

Manifested unashamedly!

In the Cross

I see the Banality

Expressed transparently!

In the Cross

I feel the Colorful-Density

Enfleshed in blood and water!

In the Cross

I find my thickly feathered,

But ruthlessly scattered,

shards of Self!

In the Cross

I see the traces of resurrection

Engraved with a Divine Beak!

3

Facing the Facelessness

The pre-text

of a face-to-face xp

is another face.

How can I gaze @

my own face

with my own eyes?

We see ourselves

through the "other"-

an inevitable post-text!

4

Virus

Virus…Virus..

Virus….Virus…

the omnipresent,

Why don't

Re-wire us?

The Edge

The edge

is significant,

when we look at the maze.

The grace

is sufficient

when we blessed with confusion.

Unchartered terrains

demand

Uncharted Journeys!

6

Travel

Where are you going my friend?

I don't know!

The Map is under my foot bro.

7

Transgression

Look,

The humanity and divinity interplay

In the childhood!

It is the time,

the only time in which

transgression is the rule!

8

Amma

In that small backyard-playground

Korean kids called their mother

Amma…,

Tamilian kids invoked,

Amma…,

& Mallu kids also called

Amma…

One single immediate reality that

Transcends our barriers-

Amma!!

Inside-Out

Where is my inside-ness

lost out there?

Where is my outside-ness

lost in here?

The re-demption of the

"inside-outside"-ness

and "outside-inside"-ness

opens my heart to

a new realm of conversations.

10

Ark

I need an ark,

pure as paper

before the poem,

to celebrate

my ostrich-moments!

to dream beyond the Niles,

to find a Moses deep within me!

Holy...Holy...Holy!

Getting "dirt"-ied by the soil,

Breathing under the water,

Touched by the sky and clouds,

Talking to the trees and birds,

Washing dishes in the sink,

Seeing colors in the soap bubbles,

Loving more after a tough talk…

All are my ways to Wholiness!

Rainbow

The sunlight

touches the edges of your skin,

trans-letting a beautiful rainbow!

Through that rainbow

tears seem jewels

on your cheeks!

13

Exit

Exits!!

They are not always well lit!

Often,

not well appreciated too,

especially when

a grand show goes on

which makes any sense

only to the luxury seats!

14

R-e-d-e-m-p-t-i-o-n

When a poor girl
takes her school bag again,
When a farmer blushes to see the first bloom,
When a priest sees
the poor guy washes his tears,
When the river
starts to flow again, ….
When we keep open
the channels of love and gift,
volunteer to support
someone less safe,
finding new ways of communicating,
even simply meditating,
asking new questions,
It happens; the r-e-d-e-m-p-t-i-o-n!

15

Porous Calendar

I always wished
to have a porous Calendar,
In which the numbers
insanely dance together,
transgressing the four tiny walls
of their boxy-homes.
Even, I tried to live out that
awesome porosity.
One day my teacher called me:
"Are you in this world?
Submit your paper exactly at 00:00."
I got enlightened;
Teachers are truly magicians
who can make us intensely-
connected to "this world!"
Bottom line:
Your time-sense is simply
your location-sense!

Silence

What is silence?
It's the time that my soul
wants to create new words
'cause,
no given words found befitting!
What is silence?
It is the energy preserved,
to burst out as a new glossia
What is silence?
It is the breathlessness
of the one,
Who has lost his language!
What is silence?
It is the womb from which
My loudest convictions explode.

17

Immanence

The soil said while I plow it;

Be gentle dear, Yesterday

I too was a human being like you!

Seed began to talk while I sow it;

Unless you plunge yourself in death,

You never know the beautiful depths!

Stem conversed when I tried to tame it;

No matter how many worlds you grow into,

You remain an earthling!

Roots rhymed in my ears, while I water it;

When the routes go wrong,

Roots must grow strong!

Leaf loved to say, while I pamper it;

Throw yourself into serendipity

It is the art of immanence!

Sky said when I sighed looking above;

Look; in-between your breaths

Eternity inhabits!

The Wood Pecker

You visited us, without notice!
until then, we never noticed you!
You were with us, but we weren't with you!
From the ashes of a crushed home,
you created a divine sanctuary within us.
And, gifted us cathedral moments.

Crushed in your memories,
bruised in your agonies,
I wonder, how you transcend
melancholy into melodies!
In the eerie nights of solitude,
dazed in the fury wind,
drenched in the misty rain,
you might have dreamt of a winged life!

No other way to guard you,
no, any word can save you!
Inside your cage,
we imbricated our world into yours,

but you graciously chirped back to us,
as a mystical river diffused!

We know, this is a matter of time
but for you, a chattel of regime.[1]
We saw your parents visit, and feed you,
but recessed for the time being.
They may be busy, building a new home;
a cutie-beauty home,
for a sublime reunion!

One day, you will trust your wings,
stand on your ground,
and burst out in your spirit,
to reach the limits of the sky,
and to chat with the stars.

Thank you for being-with,
and teaching us;
We journey each other home,
as we are the intertwined-interbeings!
Yes for sure,
the woodpecker is a bio-mystical relationship
between the wood and it's wounds!

---

[1] Referring to the chattel bodies in African American slave narratives.

God in the Backyard

My Mom had

A unique garden in the backyard!

Where;

Jasmine bloomed together with Curry leaves,

Ginger groomed with jack-fruit seeds,

Banana embraced Papaya,

Tapioca chit-chatted with Purple Yam.

Chickens danced with Crows,

And,

the Divine tryst-ed with the Mundane.

Yeah… I got it,

A Garden is a Counter-Statement!

20

Color of Breath

Some breaths are like that;

Cheaper than a toot,
Casual like Co2
bubbles up from the Coke!
Easy to be silenced,
Under the white knees!

White, Red, Yellow,
Brown, Black, Betwixt…
Yes, our breath has color,
Dear bro!
If you never noticed
Indeed, you're color blind.

On
A Pentecost day;
the day of divine breath,

It was for a worldwide sale!
The cheapo blackish sold out,
Like an alluring spectacle!
The curves, alleys,
Crossings, and stops at the red-light
uncannily resemble
branched out Lynching trees!
Strange fruits are the same!
Abysmal, abject black bodies.

Who wanna know?
Who wanna make the point?
On the top of the countless-
unbreathed blackish breaths,
The city is built, the life eructed!

Look; under your boot, a thick stench of blood!
Wherever the unbreathed-breaths suffocate,
Wherever the unsighed-sighs constellate,
Sure, there will be a Calvary or Tiananmen,
"And sooner or later,
the Tanks will appear!" [1]
Yet, We will sing the "Litanies for Oxygen."[2]

I have a Q to my Sister-folks.
And, I don't need an answer!

Don't get me wrong,
This is not a Yoga-talk
But a life & death-Query:
"When did you last have a full-length of breath?"

---

¹ Giorgio Agamben, *The coming community* (Minneapolis: University of Minnesota,2013),86.

² Indebted to my friend Fr. Patrick Saint Jean for this idiom. See his essay https://thejesuitpost.org/2020/05/after-george-floyds-suffocation-a-litany-for-oxygen-from-a-black-jesuit/

21

Re-pathing with the Farmers

Path-ing; a New Way!
For an 8 km stretch,
near Singhu Border
exactly at 28°34'38.4"N^2, Delhi
We struck by a "New Path"
For a new India!
-Eureka!

Food; a Key
The old Wiseman from the tent
invited us:
"Come and Dine!"
We embraced by
a new -"Beth-lehem"
on the road!

Religion; an Interruption

Religion?
Yes, it broke out its old cage
diffused on the road,
carried by the broken toes,
un-relinquished energy!
-"Chalo Delhi."

City; Surrounded by Villages

Finally,
The dream has come true!
A city surrounded by
The villages!
-"Ache Din!"

Weakness; as Strength

In the sweet rhymes
of those little kids
sitting back
on a tractor,
in those feeble but solid words
from that ordinary "citizen,"

on stage, and

in the slow but steady melody

poured out from that old Bulbul,

we found a "Weak Messianism!³"

---

¹ This poetic rendering is inspired by Dharma Jyoti Vidya Peeth Faculty collective solidarity-visit to the Singhu Border, where the farmers are on strike against the newly passed hegemonic-bills by the central government.

² Courtesy google map!

³ Weak messianism is an idea popularized by Walter Benjamin. Please refer to his classic work for further reading –Walter Benjamin, Illuminations, (New York: Shocken Books, 1968), 254." Theses on History," and the link below.

https://www.google com/url?sa=t&rct=j&q=&esrc=s&source=web&cd= &cad=rja&uact =8&ved=2ahUKEwiPjqjit4_uAhX6zDgGHaHtAdMQFj ACegQIAxAC&url=https%3A%2F%2Fceasefiremagazine.co.uk%2F walter-benjamin-messianism-revolution-theses-history%2F&usg=AOvVaw3VF6S W3gLv06xDhiW4TQoL

9 789390 569403